ACTS OF THE APOSTLES

And the Beginning of the Church
AD 30 - 65

EASY BIBLE SURVEY WORKBOOK

#4

Katheryn Maddox Haddad

And the Beginning of the Church

Other Books by this Author

BIBLICAL HISTORICAL NOVELS
Series of 8: Soul Journey With the Real Jesus
Ongoing Series of 8: Intrepid Men of God

CHILDREN'S BIBLE STORYBOOKS
Series of 8: A Child's Life of Christ
Series of 10: A Child's Bible Heroes
Series of 8: A Child's Bible Kids

WORLDWIDE HISTORICAL RESEARCH
DOCUMENTARY, THESIS, NOVEL & SCREENPLAY WRITERS

BIBLE TOPICS
Applied Christianity: Handbook 500 Good Works
Christianity or Islam? The Contrast
The Holy Spirit: 592 Verses Examined
Inside the Hearts of Bible Women-Reader+Audio+Leader
Revelation: A Love Letter From God
Worship Changes Since 1st Century + Worship 1st Century Way
Was Jesus God? (Why Evil)
365 Life-Changing Scriptures Day by Date
The Road to Heaven
The Lord's Supper: 52 Readings with Prayers

BIBLE FUN BOOKS
Bible Puzzles, Bible Song Book, Bible Numbers

TOUCHING GOD SERIES
365 Golden Bible Thoughts: God's Heart to Yours
365 Pearls of Wisdom: God's Soul to Yours
365 Silver-Winged Prayers: Your Spirit to God's

SURVEY SERIES: EASY BIBLE WORKBOOKS
→Old Testament & New Testament Surveys
→Questions You Have Asked-Part I & II

Genealogy: How to Climb Your Family Tree Without Falling Out
Volume I & 2: Beginner-Intermediate & Colonial-Medieval

COVER BY SHARON LAVY
Copyright © 2014 Katheryn Maddox Haddad   ISBN-978-1-952261-47-3
NORTHERN LIGHTS PUBLISHING HOUSE
This book may not be reproduced without written permission.

Acts of the Apostles

Contents

Contents iii
How to Use This Book..5
   Introduction 7

Week One
   Ch 1 Jesus' Followers Await Instructions 8
   Ch 2 First Church Sermon 10
   Ch 3 Peter Challenges Worshippers.................................15
   Ch 4 Peter Challenges Religious Leaders I....................16

Week Two
   Ch4   Peter Challenges Religious Leaders II...................18
   Ch 5 The Church's First Problem 21

Week Three
   Ch 6 Second Office of the Church Established 26
   Ch 7 Stephen Reviews Jewish History up to Jesus.........27
   Ch 8 Deacon Philip Spreads the Word I 33

Week Four
   Ch 8 Deacon Philip Spreads the Word II 36
   Ch 9 Conversion of a Future Apostle...............................37
   Ch 10 Conversion of First-Non-Jew I...............................41

Week Five
   Ch 10 Conversion of First Non-Jew II................................46
   Ch 11 Peter Defends Gentiles in Jerusalem....................46
   Ch12   Death of the First Apostle.......................................48
   Ch 13 Paul's First Missionary Trip I 51
   Ch 14 Paul's First Missionary Trip II 53

Week Six
   Ch 14 Paul's First Missionary Trip III 54
   Ch 15 Paul's First Missionary Trip IV................................55
   Ch 16 Paul's Second Missionary Trip I.............................56

Ch 17	Paul's Second Missionary Trip II	59
Ch 18	Paul's Second Missionary Trip III	61
	Paul's Third Missionary Trip I	62
Ch 19	Paul's Third Missionary Trip II	63

Week Seven

Ch 19	Paul's Third Missionary Trip III	66
Ch 21	Paul's Third Missionary Trip IV	68
Ch 22	Paul's Trial Before the Jewish Sanhedrin I	70
Ch 23	Paul's Trial Before the Jewish Sanhedrin II	70
Ch 24	Paul's Trial Before Roman Governor Felix I	72

Week Eight

Ch 24	Paul's Trial Before Roman Governor Felix II	73
Ch 25	Paul's Trial Before Roman Governor Festus	74
Ch 26	Paul's Trial Before Jewish/Roman King Agrippa	76
Ch 27	Shipwreck on the Way to Rome	77
Ch 28	Paul Arrives in Rome to be Heard by Nero	79

Thank You	81
About The Author	82
Connect With the Author	83
Buy Your Next Book Now	84

How to Use This Book

Dear Bible Student:

The Bible is easy to understand. It is people who make it complicated. These lessons are surveys, not in-depth studies.

Despite good intentions, many people in our fast-paced world today find it difficult to find time to learn the Bible. If you are one of these, this book is for you. You will be in and out of the study in no time.

The Bible has been translated into English several times. I suggest, if you do not have one, you order a New International Version (NIV) since many of the questions are fill-in-the-blank. NIVs are sold everywhere.

Dates are based on the corrected Gregorian Calendar. Therefore, Jesus was born 6 BC, two or four years before King Herod died.

The questions are easy. They go right down the line, verse by verse. Each week is subdivided into days, so you need not spend more than about ten minutes a day learning. Remember, your best learning is done when you are studying alone.

You may decide to make this a group study. Since you have already looked up all the verses in your Bible at home, it is suggested that you go through all the answers in a timely and lively manner.

But do take your Bible with you to your study group. Sometimes we misread a verse and get a wrong answer (in a hurry that day?), so those are the verses you will want to look up when together with your study group.

For further ease in study, your group leader may wish to supply you with a list of page numbers a week ahead of time for the few scriptures referred to in other parts of the Bible. If you prefer to use a Bible you already have, put a bookmark in the Table of Contents of your Bible. Most Tables of Contents are both in alphabetical order and chronological order.

Try to set aside an hour and a half for your study group. Spend your first half hour sharing your past week with each other, followed by a prayer for each other. You can go through all the questions allotted for each week in the remaining hour.

And the Beginning of the Church

Should questions arise requiring more in-depth study, write them down. Then, at the end of your eight- or ten-week study, set aside a month for them. Use a concordance or word search and look up everything the Bible has to say about that subject. That is easy to do.

I guarantee that you will learn so much in just one week that you will be thrilled. Many people using these lessons say they learn more in one week than they do in a year normally. I hope this does not describe your past, but if it does, tell yourself, "And this is just the beginning!"

Should you have a question, contact me through my website at **https://NorthernLightsPublishingHouse.com**

Acts of the Apostles

Introduction

Acts is the fifth book of the New Testament.

It follows the four accounts of the life of Christ. Every book of the New Testament was a letter personally written by one of the apostles or close associates. The four accounts of the life of Jesus were named after their authors ~ Mathew, Mark, Luke, and John.

Acts was written by the same man who had previously written a life of Jesus to Theophilus ~ Luke. Luke was a physician (see Colossians 4:14).

The full name for Acts is "Acts of the Apostles." It starts with the ascension of Jesus to heaven, and the origin of the church ten days later.

The rest of the book tells how congregations were set up and how people became Christians in the first century under the direction of the apostles. Much of it is the life of the apostle Paul, who wrote many letters/books in the New Testament by inspiration of the Holy Spirit.

The twelve apostles eventually left Jerusalem and scattered around the world to spread the saving good news of Jesus. They, undoubtedly, wrote letters to people in the nations they went to, but their writings were not preserved.

And the Beginning of the Church

Week One

Chapter 1
AD 30 - Jesus' Followers Await Instructions

DAY ONE:

VERSE 3
A letter written to the church in Corinth in Greece, much later states that Jesus appeared to over 500 people after he came back to life (1 Corinthians 15:3-8). For how many days after Jesus came back to life did he show himself to people before returning to heaven?

_____

VERSE 2-5
To whom did Jesus say they would be baptized with the Holy Spirit in a few days? _____
_____

VERSE 6-7
When the apostles asked Jesus when he would restore the kingdom of Israel, he said it was not for them to know the _____ and _____ God has decided on.

VERSE 2, 8
To whom did Jesus say they would receive power from the Holy Spirit? _____

VERSE 8
Jesus predicted that, within their lifetime, they would preach to the ends of the _____. (We will see later how the two ~ power of the Holy Spirit and the radius of their ministry ~ are connected.)

VERSE 9-11
After saying this, Jesus started rising up into the sky. Those who saw him do this were who? _____ of _____.

NOTE: Galilee was one of the provinces of Palestine at that time.

Acts of the Apostles

All the apostles were from Galilee except Judas Iscariot. (Joshua 15:25 says Kerioth was in Judah to the south) and Judas was now dead (see Matthew 26:14 and 27:5).

How will Jesus return some day? _____
_____

A letter written to the church in northern Greece—1 Thessalonians 4:17—says Christians will meet Jesus where? _____
_____

VERSE 12-13
This same group of men returned to Jerusalem to a room they were apparently renting. Compare the list of men here with the list in Matthew 10:2-4, the first book of the New Testament. As a group, these men were called the _____

DAY TWO:

VERSE 14
Who joined them in that room? _____
_____
and his _____.
What were the names of Jesus' brothers (see Matthew 13:55-56)?
_____
_____
_____

Before Jesus' crucifixion, had his brothers believed he was actually the Son of God? (See John 7:5)_____

VERSE 15-20
Jesus was crucified during Passover Week (John 19:14), and came back to life at the end of that week. Pentecost means the 50th day after Passover.

It was after the 40 days Jesus showed himself (verse 3) and during the next ten days that the apostles waited for the Holy Spirit to come to them as Jesus had told them just before ascending.

It was during those ten days before the Day of Pentecost that Peter stood among a group numbering _____

And the Beginning of the Church

and said who among the apostles should be replaced? _____
_____

VERSE 21-22
The qualifications to be an apostle wee that this person must have been with "us" the _____ time from John [the Baptist's] _____ until Jesus was _____.

VERSE 23-26
Who was chosen to take Judas' place as an Apostle? _____
_____

Chapter 2
First Church Sermon

VERSE 1
Then, on another day, what day arrived? _____
_____

Who did "they" refer to as being all together in one place?

vs. 7 _____ from _____
vs. 14 _____and the Eleven
vs 15 These _____
vs 37 Peter and the _____
_____

VERSE 2
What sound did "they" hear? _____
_____

VERSE 3
What did "they" see?_____
_____

DAY THREE:

VERSE 4
When "they" were filled with the _____
_____, they began to speak in _____
Were these known languages or unknown languages?

Acts of the Apostles

VERSE 5-8
Who was speaking so everyone could hear in their own language (verse 7)? _____ from

VERSE 9-12
How many countries were represented by the crowd who heard them speak?

1 Parthia (Iraq)	First Language
2 Media (Syria)	Second Language
3 Elam (Iran)	Third
4 Mesopotamia (Iraq)	Fourth Language
5 Judea (Palestine)	Fifth Language
6 Pontus (North Turkey)	Sixth Language
7 Asia (West Turkey)	Seventh Language
8 Cappadocia (East Turkey)	Eighth Language
9 Phrygia (SE Turkey)	"
10 Pamphylia (SC Turkey)	"
11 Egypt (N. Africa)	Ninth Language
12 Cyrene (N. Africa)	"
13 Rome (Italy)	Tenth Language
14 Crete (Greece)	Eleventh Language
15 Arabia (Arabia)	Twelfth Language

It is believed the native tongues of some of these countries were similar since they were so close to each other. In that case, how many different languages would have been spoken on that day by the twelve apostles? _____

VERSES 14-15
In that case, all twelve spoke to the crowd, which far exceeded the _____ who were saved that day (see verse 41).
However, whose sermon is recorded? _____

VERSE 17
What son of Israel had in the previous decades prophesied? (See Luke 1:11 & 67) _____
What daughter of Israel had prophesied? (See Luke 1:41-45)

And the Beginning of the Church

What young man saw visions? (See Matthew 1:19-20; Matthew 2:13 & 2:19-20) _____
What old man dreamed dreams? (See Luke 2:26-27) _____
_____

VERSE 19
What sign had appeared in the sky? (See Matthew 2:1 & 9)
_____

What sign appeared on the earth? (See Matthew 3:16-17 and Acts 2:24) _____

What sign of blood appeared? (See Matthew 26:26-29 and 27:35)
_____

What sign of fire appeared? (See Acts 2:1-4) _____
_____

VERSE 20
When had the sun turned to darkness recently? (See Luke 23:44-45) _____

VERSE 22
Jesus was authenticated or proven to be telling the truth by the
_____,
_____ and
_____ God did through him.

THOUGHT QUESTION: During whose lifetime did all these signs that had been prophesied occur? _____

VERSE 23
Peter, who denied even knowing Jesus during his trial, now put his own life on the line by accusing the crowd of what?
_____
_____

DAY FOUR:

VERSE 36
Since The Christ is a title, who did Peter say The Christ was (see also 32)?

Acts of the Apostles

_____
and _____

VERSE 37
Realizing they had murdered the Son of God, many in the crowd were _____ to the heart and begged Peter and the other apostles, "What _____ we do?"

VERSE 38
Peter replied, "_____
And be _____
_____
of you for the _____
of your _____. Then you will receive the
_____ of the _____
_____.

VERSE 39
Peter said this command and gift applied to everyone who heard him that day "and for your _____
_____, and all who are _____
_____."

Since he was referring to generations, who do you think are the people who are far off? _____

VERSE 40-41
What did those who accepted the message do that same day?
_____
How many were there who did so? _____

Since the sermon began at 9:00 AM (verse 15) and assuming the sermon ended at 10:0 AM and dark arrived about 6:00 PM, that would give _____ hours to baptize everyone. With 12 apostles and 3000 people, each apostle would have had to baptized _____ each hour, or one every two minutes. (This does not count meal breaks.)

NOTE: There were many large ornamental pools in Jerusalem.

Below is the water capacity of these pools in cubic meters. By comparison, Solomon's Pools held 8,048,400 cubic feet of water.

And the Beginning of the Church

The Serpent Pool was nearly as large as King Herod's entire palace complex.

Solomon's Pools	228,000 cubic meters
Temple Mount Pools	40,000 cubic meters
Hezekiah's Pool	30,000 cubic meters
Serpents Pool	50,000 cubic meters
Mamilla Pool	30,000 cubic meters
Bethesda Pools	90,000 cubic meters
Israel Pool	110,000 cubic meters

THOUGHT QUESTION: Do you think those baptized earlier in the day might have helped baptized people after them? In that case, would they have required someone who was "ordained" in order to make their baptism valid?

VERSE 42
Since the New Testament had not been written yet, what did the first Christians rely on to know if they were in the will of God?

_____

_____

NOTE: The word "devoted" is from a Greek word meaning "addicted."

VERSE 43
Did everyone who became saved perform miracles? _____
Who performed the miracles?_____

_____

AD 31

DAY FIVE:

VERSE 44-45
So much love developed among the believers, the first Christians, that many sold their _____ so they could give to those in _____ .

VERSE 46
Compare the breaking bread sentence in verse 42 with the breaking bread sentence in verse 46. List below the other things they did or

Acts of the Apostles

felt in connection with breaking bread, one column for verse 42 and a second column for verse 46.

_____	_____
_____	_____
_____	_____
_____	_____

Might one "breaking bread" have been for religious purposes and the other for physical health purposes? _____
(For help, read 1 Corinthians 11:23-26).

VERSE 47
What did the other people of the community think of the new Christians? _____
_____

Who made the decision whether someone was added to "the number" of the saved? _____
Who should make that decision today?_____
The new movement of Christians grew in number how often?
_____

Chapter 3
Peter Challenges Worshippers

VERSE 1
Although Peter and John were now Christians, they continued to go to the Jewish _____ to see who they could teach.

VERSE 2
At the time of their arrival, someone was carrying a severely crippled man to beg from the worshippers. He had been crippled how long? _____

VERSE 7-8
How long did it take atrophied muscles to regrow? _____
This miracle was performed by Peter, one of the original _____ (Acts 1:13).

VERSE 13-15
Note the things Peter accused these temple worshippers of doing to

And the Beginning of the Church

Jesus. List below all the phrases that Peter begins with "You...."

_____
_____
_____
_____

DAY SIX:

VERSE 17-20
Even though Peter told the crowd they had acted in _____ _____, he still told them to _____ and turn to God so their sins would be _____.

Peter said two things (two times) would occur when people repented. What are they?
_____
_____

VERSE 21
What is Peter talking about Jesus restoring? (Look back at Acts 1:6)._____
_____

What else is the kingdom called in the Bible? (Look at Colossians 1:13 and 18). _____
_____

VERSE 22-23
About 1440 BC, Moses predicted a prophet like him that "you must _____ to."

VERSE 24-25
All the _____ who lived hundreds of years
before Jesus predicted that through one of Abraham's descendants, _____ the _____ _____ on _____ would be
_____

Chapter 4
Peter Challenges Religious Leaders

Acts of the Apostles

VERSE 1-2
Who angrily approached Peter and John while they were talking to the people? _____, _____
Of the _____ _____
And the _____.

The Sadducees did not believe in what (see Matthew 22:23)?
_____

VERSE 3-4
Even though Peter and John were put in jail for preaching the resurrection, how many defied the Jewish religious leaders and believed anyway? _____

VERSE 5-6
These same elders, chief priests, and teachers had tried _____ about two months earlier (see Mark 14:53).

Their governing body was called the S_____ (Mark 14:55). Who was Ananus (see John 18:12-13)? _____

NOTE: Josephus said Ananus was appointed high priest by Rome when Jesus was about 13 years old. He held it for about three years. Then Ananus' son, Eleazar, became high priest. Caiaphas, Ananus' son-in-law, was high priest from 18-36 AD. Ananus always controlled. Ananus had five sons, and all five were high priests at some time. (*Antiquities of the Jews*)

And the Beginning of the Church

Week Two

Chapter 4 (cont.)
Peter Challenges Religious Leaders

DAY ONE:

VERSE 10
Who did Peter accuse of killing Jesus? _____
_____

Who apparently showed up in court the next morning to boldly defend Peter and John?

VERSE 11
Peter quoted David, who predicted about 1500 BC that builders would reject a stone that would be Jesus. Who did he call the builders? _____

VERSE 12
There is no other _____ under heaven by which we must be saved. That includes every other religious founder in the world.

VERSE 13-15
(See John 11:48) The Sanhedrin did not want this new Christianity to grow because they were afraid _____ would believe in Jesus, and then the _____ would _____ their jobs and perhaps even destroy their nation.

NOTE: This did happen forty years later due to their stubbornness toward the Roman government.

VERSE 16-17
The same thing that kept them from harming Peter and John at this time is what kept them from harming Jesus for so long. Look up Matthew 21:46. What was that reason? _____
_____

Acts of the Apostles

Jesus had warned just before his crucifixion that his disciples would be hated because the world _____ Jesus _____. (See John 15:18)

VERSE 18-20
When warned not to talk about Jesus any more, Peter and John replied that they would _____ and not man.

THOUGHT QUESTION: These were the religious leaders Peter and John were talking to. If religious leaders tell us something different than what Jesus said (adding to his commands or taking from his commands), should we blindly follow the religious leader?

VERSE 21-22
For how long had the healed man been lame? _____

THOUGHT QUESTION: Surely there were many in the temple that day who needed healing. Why do you think Peter and John singled out this man?

DAY TWO:

VERSE 23-24
Even church leaders need encouragement. Where did Peter and John go to when they were released? _____
_____
_____

VERSE 25-26
These followers of Jesus quoted one of the Psalms declaring that any nation that rages and plots against God do so in _____
_____.

By arresting, jailing, and harassing Peter and John, the rulers were arresting, jailing, and harassing God and his_____
_____.

NOTE: In those days, the Jews inaugurated each new high priest and crowned each new king by anointing them.

VERSE 27

And the Beginning of the Church

Herod was the governor of the province of Galilee in the north part of Palestine where Jesus lived. Pilate was the Roman governor of Judea in the southern part of Palestine where the temple was. They _____ against _____ _____ God's anointed one.

VERSE 28
The Jews executed by stoning (John 10:31). Yet, it had been prophesied centuries earlier than Jesus would be pierced (Zechariah 12:10 in the O.T.). Only the Romans had the power to pierce of crucify as a means of death. It was by God's _____ and _____ that this government would be in power when Jesus came.

VERSE 29
These early Christians knew that what people consider as threats, God can turn into his good use. Therefore they asked to help them keep spreading the word about Jesus with great _____
_____

VERSE 30
Was the purpose of healing just to heal or to accomplish something else? (Look up John 20:30 and 31)?_____
_____

VERSE 31
Because the New Testament had not been written yet, the early Christians had to rely on external things to know they were in God's will. God answered their prayer by making their meeting place
_____

DAY THREE:

VERSE 32
The believers (they were not called Christians yet) loved each other so much that no one claimed his _____ were his _____, but _____ _____ everything they had.

VERSE 33
Who was it who displayed power as they testified that Jesus came back to life?_____

VERSE 34-37
Among those who sold possessions to help out poor believers was a Jew from the island of Cyprus named _____ _____. His name means _____
_____

Who in your life is being a personal Barnabas to you? _____
_____

Chapter 5
AD 32 ~The Church's First Problem

VERSE 1
The previous chapter 4:34-37 explained how the early Christians made sure there were no needy ones in their group. This was a kind of welfare program. They sold their land from _____ to _____ (see 4:34), whenever more money was needed.

VERSE 2
Ananias and his wife, Sapphira, sold some property. But with his wife's _____ knowledge, he only took part of the money to the apostles. That made her an accessory.

VERSE 3
Apparently, Ananias had told the apostles he was bringing the full amount. Look ahead to verse 8. Who did Peter say influences people to lie? _____

Who did Jesus call the Father of Liars? (See John 8:44).
_____

VERSE 4
Then Peter said Ananias had lied, not to _____, but to _____

DAY FOUR:

VERSE 5-6

And the Beginning of the Church

How serious is lying? Look at Revelation, the last book of the Bible, 21:7-8. List the sins of the unforgiven that will bring them down to hell:

_____
_____
_____
_____
_____
_____
_____
_____

VERSE 7
How much later did wife Sapphira arrive where the apostles were?
_____

VERSE 8-10
Sapphira was stricken dead too. Why? _____
_____

VERSE 11
Does this verse say anyone dropped out of the church in Jerusalem because of God's punishment? _____

VERSE 12-13
Who continued to perform signs and wonders (miracles)?
_____
Who continued to meet in Solomon's Porch of the temple?
_____
Why do you think they met there? (Recall Acts 3:11.)
_____

NOTE: Solomon's porch was half a mile long and bordered the east boundary of the temple grounds. It could have held the thousands who had become Christians so they could worship together.

VERSE 14
Did declaring the fear of God cause people to shy away from the church? _____

Acts of the Apostles

VERSE 17
Although it never came out while Jesus was alive, apparently the High Priest Ananus was of the party of the _____ who did not believe in the _____ (Matthew 22:23)

NOTE: Josephus, the Jewish historian, said the high priest, Ananus Jr, was a Sadducee (*Antiquities of the Jews,* Book 20, 9:1). Sadducees also did not believe in the prophets in the Old Testament.

How did they feel toward the crowds following the apostles?
_____
Who else had they been jealous of just a few months earlier? (See Matthew 27:18) _____
_____

DAY FIVE:

VERSE 18-19
So, this time they arrested all the _____.
Who set them free from jail during the night? _____
_____

VERSE 20
What did the angel tell the apostles to stubbornly do? _____
_____

VERSE 21
Although they'd had a hard and eventful night, the apostles returned to the temple to talk about Jesus when? _____
_____

VERSE 22-24

NOTE: The Sanhedrin was made up of 70 men from all over the country. The original Sanhedrin was appointed two thousand years earlier by Moses (Number 11:16). In Jesus' generation, this body was corrupt.

When the Sanhedrin (Jewish Supreme Court) got to work for the

And the Beginning of the Church

next day, they sent to the _____ for the
_____, but they weren't there.

VERSE 25-26
When they learned the apostles were back in the temple, the temple guard rounded up the apostles. They did not use force on them because of who? _____

VERSE 27
Jesus had predicted the apostles would testify before local _____, and before _____, and _____ to tell about Jesus (Mark 13:9-10).

VERSE 28
The religious leaders with a false sense of righteous indignation told the apostles they were _____ to make them _____ of Jesus" blood. Were they? (Matthew 27:20 & 25) _____

DAY SIX:

VERSE 29
When confronted by the religious leaders, what did Peter and the other apostles say they MUST do? _____

VERSE 30
Rather than back down, Peter faced the most powerful ruling body among the Jews and said God brought Jesus back from death "whom _____ had _____."

VERSE 36
How many men did the rebel Theudas lead? _____

NOTE: *Theudas persuaded a great part of the people to take their effects with them and follow him to the river Jordan; for he told them he was a prophet, and that he would, by his own command, divide the river and afford them an easy passage over it; and many were deluded by his words. However, [the governor] did not permit them to make any advantage of his wild attempt, but sent a troop of*

Acts of the Apostles

horsemen out against them, who falling upon them unexpectedly, slew many of them, and took many of them alive. They also took Theudas alive, and cut off his head, and carried it to Jerusalem. This is what befell the Jews. (Josephus, Antiquities of the Jews, Book 20,k 5:1).

VERSE 37
Who else led a revolt? _____
_____

There was one Judas, a [Galilean] who became ZEALOUS to draw them to a revolt, who said that this taxation was no better than an introduction to slavery, and exhorted the nation to assert their liberty....All sorts of misfortunes also sprang from these men, and the nation was infected with this doctrine to an incredible degree; one violent war came upon us after another. (Josephus, Antiquities of the Jews, Book 28, Chapter 1, Verse 1).

VERSE 38-39
This diplomatic Gamaliel advised the Sanhedrin to let the apostles go because, if it is of _____
Origin, it will _____, but if it is from God, "You will _____ be able to stop them."

One of the few honorable men in the Sanhedrin was Gamaliel. Later on, a future apostle, Paul, said he'd grown up being taught by who? (See Acts 22:3)_____

VERSE 40-41
After being beaten and warned not to talk about Jesus any more, where did the apostles turn right around and return to?
_____
Where else did they teach? _____

NOTE: There was no stopping these apostles! Look back at your notes on Acts 2:42. These apostles were ADDICTED. They couldn't stop themselves!

A prophet 700 years earlier, Jeremiah, said this: "But if I say, "I will not mentioned him [God] or speak any more in his name," his word is in my heart like a fire, a fire shut up in my bones. I am weary of holding it in; indeed, I cannot" (Jeremiah 20:9).

And the Beginning of the Church

Week Three

Chapter 6
AD 33 ~ Second Office of the Church Established

DAY ONE:

VERSE 1
The church is made up of weak humans. If it were made up of perfect people, they wouldn't need the church. There were people living in Jerusalem of both Greek and Hebrew descent. Prejudice reared its head.

The Greek _____ were being neglected in the _____ _____ of _____.

VERSE 2
About how many members did the church in Jerusalem have by now? (See Acts 2:42 and Acts 4:4) _____

The twelve apostles were extremely busy teaching. But they knew the poor needed to be take care of too. In verse 1 above, the original Greek word translated 'distribution" in some Bibles is *"ministration"* in other Bibles. The Greek word is *diakania*. In verse 2, the original Greek word translated "wait on" or 'serve' is *diakonein.*

I Timothy 3:8-13 explains the qualifications of *diakonous* and this Greek word is translated deacon.

VERSE 3-4
Seven men were selected to serve as the first "deacons". They were known to be _____ of the Spirit and _____.

VERSE 5-6
Among the seven deacons were Stephen and Philip. We will learn more about them later.

Acts of the Apostles

What did the apostles do to these new deacons? _____
their hands on them [in a ceremonial manner, as we shall see later].

VERSE 7
The church continued to grow. In fact, a large number of _____
_____ became obedient to Jesus Christ.

THOUGHT QUESTION: Do you believe they lost their jobs by making such a stand? Could you make such a stand for Jesus?

VERSE 8
Stephen is the first man mentioned who was not an apostle who performed _____. Remember, the apostles had "laid their hands on him."

AD 34

VERSE 11-14
How did the Jews from outside of Palestine persuade some men to say Stephen had spoken against Moses and God? _____
_____
_____

Who else was condemned to die because some men were bribed to say this about him? (See Mark 14:55-59) _____
_____

DAY TWO:

VERSE 15
Suddenly Stephen's face was like the _____ of an _____ and members of the Sanhedrin started at him.

Surely the Sanhedrin should have believed when this happened. We'll find out why they did not in the next chapter. Perhaps Stephen needed this in order to face what he was about to face.

Chapter 7
Stephen Reviews O.T. Leading up to Jesus

And the Beginning of the Church

BACKGROUND: Stephen stood before the Sanhedrin and reviewed the history of the Jews to try to prove Jesus is the Savior, the King that was prophesied through Jewish prophets all those centuries. He also pointed out their stubborn ancestors who refused God's guidance. This is an excellent quick Old Testament survey.

VERSE 2
Abraham's early life was where? _____
_____

NOTE: He lived in the city of Ur. Ruins of UR have been located near where the Euphrates and Tigris Rivers join before entering the Persian Gulf. Genesis 2:14 says this meeting place of rivers was where the Garden of Eden was.

VERSE 3
God told Abraham to _____ his country and _____, and go to a land God would show him. (Remember, there were no maps in those days.)

VERSE 6-7
God predicted that Abraham's descendants would go to a country _____ theirs and be _____ and _____ for _____ years. But God would later punish that country for treating God's people badly.

(Stephen added the 30 years they were not enslaved while Joseph was alive.)

VERSE 8
Abraham's son was _____, Abraham's grandson was _____ whose name was later changed to Israel (meaning Prince of God). Israel had _____ sons who became the fathers (patriarchs) of the Jewish nation. Their families were so big, they were called tribes.

VERSE 9-10
Abraham's great grandson, Joseph, was sold as a _____ _____ to Egypt, but later was made _____ _____ of Egypt by _____.

VERSE 11-16

Acts of the Apostles

During a famine, Joseph's brothers went to Egypt to get
_____. After their reunion and forgiveness,
Joseph sent for his father _____ to move
there. Including his brothers' families, how many (the original Jewish
nation) moved to Egypt? _____

DAY THREE:

VERSE 17-20
After Joseph and his memory died, Egypt's Pharaohs dealt more
and more _____ with the Jews.

Eventually, fearing the Jews' growing population, the Egyptians
even killed their _____. During this time,
_____ was born.

VERSE 21-22
Moses was adopted by _____
_____ and educated with the
_____.

VERSE 23-25
When Moses was _____ years old, he killed an _____
_____ for mistreating a
_____. He thought the Jews would
understand he was trying to _____ them.

VERSE 26-28
Instead, the Jews didn't trust him, and thought he'd want to
_____ them too.

VERSE 29
When Moses realized it was known he'd killed an _____
_____, he went into exile in what
country? _____ (This country is
today's Arabia.) While there, Moses married and had _____
sons.

VERSE 30-33
After another _____ years, God spoke to Moses out of a
_____ bush near Mount
_____. (Later at that same mountain,

And the Beginning of the Church

God would give Moses the Ten Commandments ~ Exodus 19:18 and chapter 20).

150 years from the promise to Abraham until the death of Joseph.
200 years of slavery.
40 years for Moses to grow up.
40 years for Moses to live in and learn the wilderness that he will lead the Jews through someday.

Now, the 430 years predicted to Abraham were up.

VERSE 34
God had _____ the oppression all along. God had _____ their groanings all alone. Now God was ready.

Exodus 12:37 said there were now 600,000 Jewish men at this time. Doubling this for wives would be 1,200,000. Multiplying 4 children per couple would give over 4,000,000 Jews by this time.

THOUGHT QUESTION: God had heard their prayers all along. But they were not strong enough yet. Many died back in Egypt, believing their prayers had not been answered. They were answered in a much better way generations later. Are you praying for something you don't think God is answering?

DAY FOUR:

VERSE 35
But Moses objected, saying his people had _____ him. God insisted he lead them out of Egypt anyway.

VERSE 36
These Jews had minds of slaves (and complained all the time) and worshippers of Egyptian gods. God had to have time to teach them to think for themselves and stand up for right. So God gave the Jews time to develop a new generation. This lasted for _____ years.

VERSE 37-38
Moses predicted to the Jews, "God will send you a _____ _____ like me" (Deuteronomy 18:18-19).

Acts of the Apostles

NOTE: Just as Moses had officially started the new earthly nation of the Jews, giving it the laws to go by, there would someday be a prophet who would start a new spiritual nation of God.

John 14:5 indicates early believers recognized Jesus to be the prophet Moses had predicted.

VERSE 39-41
The first generation of Jews who left slavery in Egypt was still too influenced by Egypt. They actually told Aaron, Moses' brother, to _____ to lead them. So they made an idol that looked like a _____

NOTE: The Hindu religion still reveres/worships cows.

VERSE 44
Under Moses' direction, the _____ was made according to God's pattern. These minute directions are found in Exodus 35-40. It was a large tent. Its contents were overlaid with sheets of pure gold. They worshipped in this tent structure until the time of David and Solomon (see verse 45).

VERSE 45
It was General _____ who finally led the Jews into the Promised Land, taking it from the nations God
_____
_____

NOTE: Wasn't it cruel for God to have the Jews kill all those people and take their land from them?

ANSWER: The reason God waited 430 years to give the land to Abraham's descendants was because "the sins of the Amorites had not yet reached their full measure" (Genesis 15:16).

Further, God through Moses said that, just as God drove out the inhabitants before the Jews because of their sins, God would drive out the Jews from the same land if they committed the same sins (Leviticus 18::24-28). The sins were idol worship, including human sacrifices and sexual immorality. Indeed, the Jews were later driven out for that same reason.

And the Beginning of the Church

2nd Kings 17:17 says, "They sacrificed their sons and daughters in the fire. They practiced divination and sought omens and sold themselves to do evil in the eyes of the Lord, arousing his anger."

VERSE 46-50
David's son, King _____, replaced the old tent place of worship –the tabernacle— with a stone place of worship, the temple.

With all our beautiful church buildings today, does God actually dwell in them? Where does God dwell? (See Ephesians 1:22-23 and 2:20-22)_____

DAY FIVE:

VERSE 51-52
Finally, Stephen recalled all the Jews through the centuries who _____ and _____ the Old Testament _____ for teaching truth.

Then he pointed his finger at the Sanhedrin and said, "_____ have betrayed and murdered" the righteous One predicted by those prophets.

VERSE 55-57
Stephen probably knew they would kill him for defaming them. He had to be brave. Since the New Testament had not been written yet and he did not have that to call to memory in difficult times, what did God do to encourage him?

_____
_____
_____

Colossians 3:1 says Jesus is _____ at the right hand of God. But, watching the courage of Stephen, Jesus in heaven did what? _____

Perhaps like a general saluting a private? An admiral saluting a seaman?

VERSE 58

Acts of the Apostles

An inconspicuous young man held everyone's coats so they could _____ Stephen. His name was _____ Later in Acts, he was converted, and still later became an apostle.

THOUGHT QUESTION: Does that give you hope for friends or relatives who are right now defying God?

VERSE 59
As they began stoning him, Stephen prayed the same thing Jesus had said on the cross. Look up Luke 23:46. What did they both say?
_____
_____

Chapter 8
Deacon Philip Spreads the Word

VERSE 1-2
Saul approved of Stephen's what? _____
On that day, a great _____ broke out against the church. Christians scattered. Only the _____ _____ stayed in Jerusalem.

VERSE 3
Determined to completely _____ the church was the young man named _____ who went _____ to _____ dragging off men and _____ and putting them in _____.

AD 35

DAY SIX:

VERSE 4-5
Philip, one of the Christians who fled Jerusalem, was one of the original what in the church? (See Acts 6:5.) _____
_____

VERSE 6-8

And the Beginning of the Church

Philip got the power to perform miracles in the same way Stephen had. What was it? (See Acts 6:6.) _____
_____
_____

Some people today take to themselves the title of apostles. 2nd Corinthians 12:12 says the mark of an apostle included what?
_____
_____
_____
_____

In Acts 1:20-21, Peter declared someone else had to take Judas' place. List the qualifications of an apostle listed in verses 22

1. Had been with them since the _____ of John
2. ...until the day _____ was taken from them.
3. And been a witness of Jesus' _____.

Does anyone today meet the qualifications of an apostle?

VERSE 12-13
Many people in Samaria, along with Simon _____
_____ and were _____

VERSE 14-17
Sometime later, perhaps months, when the apostles in Jerusalem heard that the Samaritans in the province of Samaria had been converted, who was sent to them?
_____

In Matthew 28:19 Jesus commanded that people be baptized in the name of the _____, the _____, and the _____.

Peter himself had said in the first gospel sermon (Acts 2:38) that, upon baptism, they would receive the gift of the _____
_____

But these Samaritan people hadn't understood that, and had omitted being baptized in the name of the _____
_____.

Acts of the Apostles

So, when the apostles learned that, rather than have them be baptized again, the apostles laid their _____ on them (just like they had the deacons in Acts 6) and they received the Holy Spirit.

VERSE 18-25
Although verse 13 specified that Simon truly believed and was baptized, when he tried to buy the power the apostles had to give the _____ _____, Peter said his attitude was going to cause him and his money to do what?
_____
_____

Although Simon was perishing, Peter told him all he had to do was _____ to receive God's _____. He did not have to be baptized all over again.

AD 36

VERSE 26-27
Then Philip moved on to teach elsewhere. On the road, he met a _____ from Ethiopia

VERSE 28-31
Sitting in his chariot, resting, he was reading which Old Testament book? _____

Because the New Testament had not been written yet, explaining how the Old Testament had been fulfilled in Jesus Christ, this man did not understand the prophet Isaiah unless someone _____ it to him.

Romans 10:1-2 says people cannot be saved if they only have zeal for God. Their zeal must be based on what? _____

Romans 10:8 & 17 say we must believe to be saved, and belief comes from _____ (or reading) the _____ of _____

And the Beginning of the Church

Week Four

Chapter 8 (cont.)
Deacon Philip Spreads the Word

DAY ONE:

VERSE 32-35
The treasurer was reading the Old Testament, Isaiah 53:7-8, where it says a man was led like a sheep to the _____ _____.

John 1:29 says, "Behold, the _____ of God who takes away the _____ of the world.

Mark 14:61 says that, at Jesus' trial, he remained _____

NOTE: Back in Isaiah 53, verse 5, it predicts this lamb will be pierced for our sins. The Jews did not execute someone by piercing them. They stoned them.

There are many prophecies in Isaiah about Jesus, all written about 700 years before Jesus was born. Jesus couldn't possibly have purposely caused everything to happen in his life that had been prophesied unless he had been the Son of God.

VERSE 36
Suddenly, a pond appeared in the middle of the desert. After being taught by Philip, the treasurer wanted to be what?
_____

VERSE 37-40
To accomplish this, both Philip and the treasurer went _____ _____ into the _____.
Then they came _____ _____ of the _____.

Look at Romans 6:4. Do you see a comparison? What?
_____

Acts of the Apostles

Chapter 9
AD 37 ~ Conversion of a Future Apostle

VERSE 1
Saul was still trying to destroy the church by threatening to have Christians _____.

VERSE 3-4
Near Damascus, a _____ suddenly flashed around Saul. Then a voice said, "Saul! Saul! Why are you _____?"

VERSE 5
Shocked, Saul wanted to know who this "me" was. He called him _____, but couldn't figure out who he was persecuting that represented his Lord.

In Acts 22:3 where Saul (called Paul by the non-Jews) recalled this event many years later, he said he was very _____ _____. But he was still wrong ~ sincere, but sincerely wrong.

Romans 10:1-2 says we can be lost if we have a zeal for God, but it is not based on _____ of (see Romans 10:17) _____

VERSE 6
Jesus told Saul to go on into Damascus and it would be told him what he _____ do. His instructions in Damascus were not something he could do if he wanted to, or if his parents had done it before him, or if his friends or religious leaders did. These were things Jesus told him he _____ Do.

DAY TWO:

VERSE 7-9
The light _____ Saul. He stayed

And the Beginning of the Church

that way in Damascus for _____ days.

VERSE 10-14
In Damascus, Jesus appeared to _____ (not the same Christian who died earlier). Jesus told this Ananias to do what for Saul? _____
_____

Ananias objected. He'd heard many reports about Saul and all the _____ he had done to God's people.

THOUGHT QUESTION: Why do you think Ananias objected? Do we object to God for the same reason at times? If we know someone who is downright mean or who preaches against truths in the Bible, do we tell God he will never listen to you?

VERSE 15
Amazingly, Jesus said Saul, the Christian killer, was his _____ _____ to carry Jesus before the _____ and their _____ as well as to the Jews.

VERSE 16
Now that Saul had caused Christians to suffer, Jesus was going to make Saul _____. Years later, Saul/Paul would write to the Grecian Christians in Corinth (2 Corinthians 11:23-29) that he had worked much harder, been in _____ _____ more frequently, been _____ more severely and been exposed to _____ again and again. He had also been beaten with a whip _____ times, beaten with rods _____ times, been stoned _____ times, was shipwrecked _____ times, floated around in the open sea a _____. He'd been in danger from rivers, bandits, and hypocrites. He'd labored without sleep, knew _____ _____ and had been old and _____ _____.

Yet, just before his death years later, Saul/Paul wrote his friend in 2 Timothy 4:6-9, "The time has come for my _____

Acts of the Apostles

_____. I have _____ the _____ fight. I have _____ the _____. I have _____ Now there is in store for me the _____."

THOUGHT QUESTION: Is there someone you've been praying for a long time whose negative traits could be put to work by God as a positive trait?

VERSE 17-19
What things happened to Saul after Ananias arrived?
_____
_____

What things did Paul do then?
_____
_____
_____

AD 38

VERSE 20-22
The courageous Christians in _____ agreed to meet with Saul.

NOTE: In Galatians 1:16-17, Saul/Paul said he then went to Arabia, where Jesus taught him personally, and also to study the scriptures and all the prophecies that Jesus fulfilled.

Then he returned to Damascus. When Saul announced he now believed Jesus really was the Son of God, how did the people of Damascus react? _____
_____

VERSE 26
NOTE: In Galatians 1:18-19, Saul/Paul explained that it was three years after his conversion before he went to Jerusalem. It was apparently a secret visit because he saw only Peter, staying with him 15 days, and also James, Jesus' brother.

In Acts 22:17-21, Saul/Paul later recalled that they went to the

And the Beginning of the Church

temple to pray and while there Jesus told him, "Quick! Leave Jerusalem _____, because they will not accept your testimony about me." Then he reminded Saul he was supposed to preach to the Gentiles (non-Jews).

Although after Stephen's execution, all the disciples left Jerusalem except the twelve apostles, some disciples seem to have returned. These disciples were _____ of Saul, so they wouldn't let Saul _____ them.

Sometime later, _____ accompanied Saul/Paul to Jerusalem. Remember him from Acts 4:36? What does his name mean? _____

DAY THREE:

VERSE 27
NOTE: In Galatians 1:19, Saul/Paul explained that later, the only apostles apparently left in Jerusalem by then were Peter and James, Jesus' brother.

What man, whom everyone trusted, convinced the apostles and disciples to believe Saul was truly converted? _____
_____

VERSE 28-30
So Saul began preaching in Jerusalem. But some Jews tried to _____ him, so the Christian brothers sent Saul back to his hometown of _____ (see verse 11) up in Syria near Turkey.

NOTE: Apparently, Saul stayed in Tarsus (where he had been born) for a while, possibly until the first Gentile convert, which we will see shortly.

AD 40

VERSE 32
Peter didn't always stay in Jerusalem. He went to visit the saints in _____ a city near Joppa on the Mediterranean coast.
Were these saints living or dead Christians? _____

Acts of the Apostles

Where else were there saints (see verse 13)? _____
_____

VERSE 35
What did the single miracle of healing Ae-neaus cause people to do? _____

THOUGHT QUESTION: Peter didn't go to all the hospitals to heal people. He had the power to do so. Why didn't he? (Hint: John 20:30-31). _____
_____
_____

VERSE 36-39
In the town of _____ near Lydda was a woman named _____ who helped the _____ and she died. Was it before or after she died that the disciples sent for Peter to come?
_____

VERSE 40-43
Peter raised her from the _____. As a result, many people _____ in the _____. Then he moved into the home of _____ to stay awhile for follow up.

Chapter 10
AD 42 ~ Conversion of First-Non-Jew

VERSE 1
Cornelius was a _____ of the Italian Regiment. He was a captain over 100 soldiers.

DAY FOUR

VERSE 2 His name was Roman, his position was Roman, yet he and his family believed in _____, he _____ to those in need, and _____ _____ often.

And the Beginning of the Church

VERSE 3-4
One day an _____ appeared to him saying his _____ and _____ to the _____ were a _____ offering before _____.

VERSE 5-6
The angel told him to send someone to find _____ and bring him to Cornelius _____

VERSE 7-8
Who did Cornelius confide in to explain an angel had actually appeared to him? _____
_____

VERSE 9-10
In the meantime, the next day at _____ Peter went to a rooftop to _____. He became _____, but while the meal was being prepared downstairs, what happened? _____
_____
_____

VERSE 11-14
Out of _____ came a large sheet containing all kinds of _____ and _____, and _____ _____. Then a voice from heaven told Peter to do what with them? _____
_____
Did Peter argue with the Lord or obey him? _____

NOTE: In the Law of Moses (Leviticus 11:1-31) their diet was explained. (Yes, there were more than 10 Commandments in the Law of Moses.) The Jews could eat some four-footed animals, but couldn't eat camels or pigs. Of birds, they could not eat eagles or vultures. Of reptiles, they couldn't eat rats or lizards. When you analyze all the "unclean" animals, they are all scavengers and are bad for one's health.

VERSE 15
God replied that he had now made these animals _____

Acts of the Apostles

_____

DAY FIVE:

VERSE 16
How many times did Peter and God argue? _____

VERSE 17
Peter realized this vision had some kind of _____
_____, but didn't yet know what.

VERSE 18-20
In the meantime, Cornelius' messengers arrived. God indirectly told Peter the meaning of his vision by telling him to do what?
_____
_____

VERSE 22
The messengers explained to Peter that Cornelius was God-fearing and respected by what nationality? _____
_____ (another indication he was not a Jew).

VERSE 23
When Peter invited these people into his house to be his _____
_____, he was going against every Jewish tradition. Since it was noon, he probably ate with them too. Then he even spent the night there! (A good Jew would have never done this with a gentile.)

VERSE 24
The next day, Cornelius, expecting Peter, invited who to come to his house? _____
_____

VERSE 25
When Peter arrived, what did Cornelius do? _____
_____

DAY SIX:

VERSE 26
What was Peter's reaction, and why? _____

And the Beginning of the Church

THOUGHT QUESTION: If the actual apostle of Jesus would not allow this, what do you think of self-proclaimed church leaders allowing this?

VERSE 27-29
Peter reminded the people that it was against Jewish _____ _____ to do what with Gentiles? _____
Peter then explained the meaning of his vision. What was it?
_____

VERSE 36-38
Peter tried to prove Jesus was really the Son of God by explaining that he had performed _____.

VERSE 39-40
Although Jesus was then crucified, Peter explained that on the third day, he did what? _____

VERSE 42-43
Peter then gave another proof of Jesus' divinity by explaining he had fulfilled _____. Being the Son of God, he could forgive _____.

VERSE 44
Only one other time did the Holy Spirit come spontaneously on a group of people without them having to do something first. Look back at Acts 2:1-4. The first time it happened was to the apostles on the Day of _____
when the church began with the Jews.

VERSE 45
The emphasis at this time was that the Holy Spirit had been poured out on what nationality? _____

The first time, the Holy Spirit was poured out on Jews. Did the Holy Spirit come on these people before baptism mean they were already saved?

There was in earlier centuries a pagan prophet named Balaam who practiced sorcery. Yet, "the Spirit of God came upon him and he uttered his oracle" (Numbers 24:1-3) in favor of God's people. We know that, after this event, he went back to prophesying evil, and he was not saved (Joshua 13:22; 2 Peter 2:15; Revelation 2:14).

VERSE 46
Since the Jews heard all the Gentiles praising God, were there any babies present?

Now, not only the Jewish apostles, but also these Gentiles could know and speak the Truth, the Word of God (see John 14:17 and 17:17).

And the Beginning of the Church

Week Five

Chapter 10 – (cont.)
Conversion of First Non-Jew

DAY ONE:

VERSE 46
Since this event was a duplicate of what happened in Acts 2, were the tongues they spoke unknown or understood by people of other languages? _____

Look up Revelation 5:9. The same Greek word for "tongue" in Acts is used in this passage. Is it referring to "unknown" or what is used by different nationalities? _____

VERSE 47
Peter challenged his companions, asking if anyone dared now keep these _____ (Gentiles) from being _____ with _____.

VERSE 48
What did Peter order them to do? _____
_____

What did this accomplish for them (see Acts 2:38)? _____
_____
_____

Chapter 11
Peter Defends Gentiles in Jerusalem

VERSE 1-3
Word spread fast about Peter allowing _____
Into the church. So, when he returned to Jerusalem, what did the Jewish believers do to him? _____

VERSE 13-14
The angel had told Cornelius that Peter would tell him and his household
how to be _____.

Acts of the Apostles

VERSE 15
Notice, Peter said the Holy Spirit came on the Gentiles as he had come on "us" on what special day? _____
_____

According to Acts 2:1, who were the "us" who received the Holy Spirit and could speak in other languages (see also Acts 1:2-5)?
_____

VERSE 16
Peter finally understood what Jesus had said when he'd told them years earlier they would be baptized with the what? _____
_____

THOUGHT QUESTION: Do you ever read a scripture but not catch on to it until years later? Has this happened to you recently?

DAY TWO:

VERSE 17
Peter then told the assembly, "Who was I to _____
_____God?"

VERSE 18
The entire book of Romans talks about both Jews and Gentiles needing Jesus because everyone has sinned (Romans 3:23).

AD 44

VERSE 19-21
In the meantime, the Christians who scattered after the martyrdom of _____ went everywhere telling others the good news about who? _____

VERSE 22
News of this reached the church where? _____
How could the church in Jerusalem have authority to tell Barnabas to go to Antioch up in Syria. Acts 6:2 says the Jerusalem congregation was led by the _____ Since we do not have apostles today, can one congregation tell another congregation what to do? _____

And the Beginning of the Church

VERSE 23-24
What did Barnabas do in Antioch? _____
_____
What kind of man was Barnabas? _____
_____

VERSE 25
Then Barnabas went where to look for who? _____
_____

VERSE 26
Saul/Paul had been a Christian for about four years by now. So Barnabas teamed up with him and together they taught the church in Antioch for how long? _____

It is in Antioch that the disciples, the believers in Jesus Christ, were called what for the very first time? _____

THOUGHT QUESTION: Do you believe this is the name BELIEVERS should use today?

DAY THREE:

VERSE 27-28
During this year, a prophet named _____ predicted there would be a severe _____ throughout the _____ world during the reign of Caesar _____.

VERSE 29-30
So the Christians in Antioch decided to provide help, each according to their____ _____. Their donations were sent to the elders in Jerusalem by whom? _____ and _____.

Chapter 12
Death of the First Apostle

Acts of the Apostles

VERSE 1
King Herod decided to arrest who? _____
_____

NOTE: There were several Herods at this time. Herod was a family name. Herod the Great ordered all the boy babies killed when Jesus was born. His son, Herod Antipas, ordered John the Baptist to be beheaded. Herod Antipas was the governor of one-fourth of Palestine and his brother, Herod Philip, was the governor of another one-fourth of Palestine.

Herod Agrippa was Herod the Great's grandson, and Antipas' and Philip's nephew through a dead brother. He was not a governor like his uncles; he was a minor king. He had a son, Herod Agrippa Jr., and daughters Bernice and Drucilla, who were involved in the trial of Paul toward the end of Acts.

VERSE 2
This young King Herod had the apostle _____,
brother of the apostle _____, executed.

NOTE: James was the first of the apostles to die His brother, John, was the last of the apostles to die. (John wrote the book of Revelation, the last book in the Bible, and other books named after him.)

VERSE 1-5
Who did James' death please? _____
Rising in popularity, King Herod decided next to arrest who?

_____

VERSE 6
The night before his trial, which surely would have led to his death as it had James, Peter was doing what?

_____

List the things/people that kept Peter securely behind bars:
_____
_____
_____

VERSE 7

And the Beginning of the Church

Who suddenly awoke Peter? _____
What happened to his chains? _____

DAY FOUR

VERSE 8-11
What did the angel lead Peter past?
_____
_____

VERSE 12
Peter then went to the house of Mary, the mother of John _____.

NOTE: This is the same man who wrote one of the four lives of Christ and whom we call Mark. Because the book sounds so much like Peter's writings, many believe John Mark got much of his information from Peter (See I Peter 5:13)

VERSE 13-16
When Rhoda went to see who was knocking on the door in the middle of the night while everyone prayed for Peter's life, she couldn't believe it was _____ standing there in answer to their prayers.

VERSE 17
Peter told them to be sure and tell _____ what happened.

Since the apostle by this name had just been executed, which James did he probably mean? (See Galatians 1:19)

VERSE 18-20
King Herod Agrippa then went to his palace in Caesarea on the seacoast, a city his grandfather had built and named after Caesar. He'd been _____ with some people nearby, so they decided to flatter him in order to obtain _____ _____ with him.

VERSE 21-22
Herod delivered a _____, and they responded that he was surely a _____.

Acts of the Apostles

VERSE 23
Herod did not deny it. Immediately he was in pain and died of a disease wherein he was _____ by _____.

DAY FIVE:

VERSE 24
The church continued to _____.
Barnabas and _____ got their benevolent money delivered to _____. Then they asked John _____ to leave Jerusalem with them.

Chapter 13
AD 46 ~ Paul's First Missionary Trip

VERSE 1-3
The Holy Spirit told the Christians in Antioch to set apart which two men for a special work? _____
and _____.

VERSE 6-7
On the island of Cyprus, there was a _____ prophet who was personal attendant to the proconsul.

Acts 19:38 indicates that proconsuls were judges. A consul in Rome at that time was an important political leader of the empire. Proconsuls were senators and often sent to rule one part of the empire.

VERSE 8
Apparently, this proconsul was thinking seriously of becoming a Christian, for the false prophet tried to turn him from _____.

VERSE 9
Now that Saul was primarily among Gentiles, he was no longer called Saul, but rather _____.

And the Beginning of the Church

VERSE 10-11
Paul had the power to perform miracles because God had made him an apostle.

See 1 Corinthians 15:8-9 explaining this. _____
_____
_____
_____

NOTE: Thus far, the only Christians able to perform miracles were apostles or someone an apostle "laid his hands on."

Paul made Elymas _____. Had Paul himself being made blind years earlier helped Paul turn to Jesus? _____ Does it look like it helped Elymas? _____

AD 47

VERSE 12-31
Back on the mainland in Antioch, Turkey (a different Antioch from their home congregation in Syria), Paul reviewed Jewish history.

NOTE: This Antioch was in the county of Pisidia within the province of Galatia.

DAY SIX:

VERSE 32-41
Paul preached a sermon in a synagogue and concluded by showing how Jesus" life had _____ one prophecy after another.

VERSE 42-45
Everyone was so excited about this, that the next Sabbath almost the whole _____ gathered to hear Paul. But the Jews tried to outshout him because they were _____.

VERSE 46
At this point, Paul made a dynamic decision. He said he had spoken to the Jews _____, but, since they _____ God's Word, Paul was from now

Acts of the Apostles

on going to turn to the _____
people.

VERSE 50
Even more angry, the Jews stirred up the local government leaders until Paul and Barnabas were _____ from their region.

Chapter 14
AD 48 ~ (Paul's First Missionary Trip-cont.)

VERSE 5
At the next city, Iconium in Turkey, many believed. But both Gentiles and Jews plotted to _____ Paul and Barnabas, so they left.

VERSE 12-13
In Lystra, Turkey, they healed a man born lame, so the people decided they were _____, calling Barnabas by the name of _____, and Paul _____

VERSE 14-15
When Paul and Barnabas realized what was happening, they rushed through the crowd shouting, "We are only _____ like you."

And the Beginning of the Church

Week Six

Chapter 14 – cont.)
(Paul's First Missionary Trip)

DAY ONE:

VERSE 16-18
They tried to explain that the only God was the one who bought them _____ and happiness.

VERSE 19
But the Jews from the previous city had followed Paul and Barnabas here. They stirred up the people so that they _____ Paul and left him for _____.

VERSE 20
Instead, stubborn Paul got up and did what remarkable thing?
_____

AD 49

VERSE 23
Then Paul and Barnabas returned through the cities where they had started churches in earlier. At that time, they appointed _____ in each _____. (Notice, they were elders – plural. Also, no elder in one church was put in charge of other churches.)

NOTE: The cities of Derbe, Lystra, Iconium, and Antioch were all in the Turkish Roman province of Galatia. About AD 51, Paul wrote them, and it is part of our New Testament today. In Galatians 1:8-9, he made this warning:

"But even if we or an angel from heaven should preach a gospel other than the one we preached to you, let him be eternally condemned! As we have said already, so now I say again: If anybody is preaching to you a gospel other than what you accepted, let him be eternally condemned."

Acts of the Apostles

Chapter 15
AD 50 ~ (Paul's First Missionary Trip-cont.)

VERSE 1
After returning to Antioch in Syria to report the results of their missionary trip, some Christians showed up teaching that Gentile Christians had to be circumcised as the Law of Moses commanded the Jews.

AD 51

VERSE 2
So Paul and Barnabas went to Jerusalem to confer with the _____ and elders there. (Remember, they still did not have the New Testament written yet, so they had to rely on what the apostles decided.)

NOTE: This occurred _____ years after Paul's conversion. (See Galatians 2:1)

VERSE 10-11
At the Council in Jerusalem, Peter got up and said they shouldn't put a _____ on the Gentiles that the Jews couldn't even keep. Therefore, they decided Gentiles need not be circumcised because they are saved through _____.

THOUGHT QUESTIONS: Some people today have begun incorporating Jewish worship from the Old Testament into Christian worship Do you think it is important enough to look up our forms of worship in the Bible to see if they are from the Old Testament or New Testament?

Do we tend to do things in our worship that we like doing or what God likes us to do? Do we search the scriptures to find out?

DAY TWO:

VERSE 13, 20
James, the brother of Jesus, suggested they send a letter around

And the Beginning of the Church

with Paul warning Gentile Christians to abstain from what?
_____
_____
_____
_____

VERSE 23
How careful were the apostles that their instruction not be misunderstood? _____
_____

VERSE 25-27
Even though the letter was sent with Paul and Barnabas from the apostles to the church in Antioch, Syria, what further care did the Apostles take that this letter was authentic? _____
_____

THOUGHT QUESTION: The only example in the New Testament church of any group of church leaders being in charge of another congregation is this one in Jerusalem. How were the leaders in Jerusalem unique from all the others?

NOTE: This is the last we hear of the original twelve apostles being together in Jerusalem. They seem to have scattered after this. The next time the church leadership in Jerusalem is mentioned, this congregation is headed by James and elders (see Acts 21:18).

VERSE 40
Then Paul and Barnabas decided to make a second missionary trip, revisiting the areas where they'd preached before. But this time, Paul chose _____ as his preaching partner.

Chapter 16
Paul's Second Missionary Trip

VERSE 1-2
In Lystra, Turkey, Paul met who? _____
What was his nationality? _____
Were there "believers" in his family besides himself? _____

LYSTRA was not a very culturally advanced community. But two

statues have been discovered there of Zeus and Hermes.
Look up 2 Timothy 1:4. What were Timothy's mother's and grandmother's names? _____
_____ Were they Christians? _____

THOUGHT QUESTION: Who in Timothy's family do you think raised him to be a believer?

Look up 2 Timothy 1:2 & 4; also 4:9. How close did Paul and Timothy eventually become? _____
_____

NOTE: 2 Timothy is the last known letter that Paul wrote. In 1:8 he told Timothy not to be ashamed of Jesus or ashamed that Paul was a prisoner.

In 4:6 he said he would die soon (to be executed by Nero). He wanted Timothy to be with him at that time.

AD 52

VERSE 9-10
They had apparently decided to preach only in today's Turkey, but one night Paul had a vision of a man in Macedonia, a northern province of Greece. What did the man say in the vision?
_____
_____

THOUGHT QUESTION: Have you had any "Macedonians" interfere with your life and cause you to change?

VERSE 12
They went to which leading city of Macedonia? _____

NOTE: This city had a famous school of medicine. About 15 years after this visit, Paul wrote the church here while he was in prison. It was probably his most gentle letter. In Philippians 4:7, he wished them "the peace that passes all understanding," and in 4:13 he said, "I can do all things through Christ who strengthens me."

DAY THREE:

And the Beginning of the Church

VERSE 13-15
There, Paul met a business woman named _____.
After hearing Paul, what did she and her household do? _____
_____

VERSE 16-18
Paul and Silas were hounded by a psychic who kept following them around and shouting what? _____
_____
_____

THOUGHT QUESTION: Why do you think Paul caused the psychic spirit to leave her? _____
_____

VERSE 23
The woman's owners got mad because they'd made a lot of money off her. So they caused what to happen to Paul and Silas?
_____
_____

VERSE 25
What did Paul and Silas do while in prison?
_____
_____

NOTE: They had a "captive audience" and took advantage of the situation to preach through their singing.

VERSE 26-27
When the earthquake broke open the prison doors, what did the jailer threaten to do? _____
_____ because he thought the prisoners had
_____

VERSE 31-33
When the jailer asked what to do to be saved, (a) what did Paul tell him to do, and (b) what did they do?
_____
_____

Acts of the Apostles

VERSE 37-39
When the local magistrate decided to free Paul and Silas, Paul objected because:

_____
_____
_____

Chapter 17
AD 53 ~ (Paul's Second Missionary Trip-cont.)

DAY FOUR:

VERSE 1
What was the next city they went to? _____

NOTE: Paul wrote two letters to the Christians at this Grecian seaport city.

The first letter was written about AD 54. In 1 Thessalonians 4:16-17, he said, "For the Lord himself will come down from heaven with a loud command, with the voice of the archangel and with the trumpet call of God, and the dead in Christ will rise first. After that, we who are still alive and are left will be caught up together with them in the clouds to meet the Lord in the air [not anywhere on earth]. And so we will be with the Lord forever."

Paul wrote his second letter to them shortly after the first to follow up on the first letter.

VERSE 6
It is about 23 years since Jesus returned to heaven. And yet, the mob shouted that these men had caused trouble where?

_____

VERSE 7
The mob claimed Paul was defying Caesar by saying _____ Was king.

THOUGHT QUESTION: In what way do opponents of Jesus today twist around the Truth to make it sound like Christians are bad?

And the Beginning of the Church

VERSE 10-11
They escaped Thessalonica and fled to what city next? _____
Paul said these Christians were more _____ than some other Christians because they did what and how often?
_____
_____

VERSE 16
Paul then escaped to Athens, still in Greece, but was disturbed to see so many what there? _____

VERSE 18
EPICUREANS founded about 300 BC. Nature is the true reality. As atheists, they believed mind is just matter in motion. They sought happiness through pleasure. There was no such thing as absolute truth. However, they did believe in a universal morality because it ultimately leads to happiness. Man's soul is part of the soul of the world.

STOICS founded in 280 BC. Reason/Mind is the true reality. As pan-theists, they believed the laws of nature are from the Great Reason of the Universe, a Mind with no personality. Happiness was attained by eliminating emotions and just going along with nature. They believed they could best do this by being kind to others, thus alleviating conflict in their lives. Sin was just an error in judgment. The philosophers accused Paul of introducing _____
_____

VERSE 19
AR-EOP-AGUS was a stone plateau on Mars Hill in Greece. Court was held there, reportedly from legendary times, and still was in Paul's time. Its purpose was to question the morals and rights of teachers who lectured in public. They also voted on who to declare gods.

DAY FIVE:

VERSE 32
After Paul testified of Jehovah God, many of them sneered because he believed in what? _____
_____

VERSE 34

Acts of the Apostles

Only a few in Athens believed, among them a member of the
_____, and a woman named
_____.

Chapter 18
A 54 ~ (Paul's Second Missionary Trip-cont.)

VERSE 1
Paul next went to what city? _____

NOTE: This city had a major temple to Aphrodite that housed 1000 prostitutes. They also worshipped Poseidon, the god of the sea, since this was a seaport. The city had over twice as many slaves as citizens.

Paul wrote the church in Corinth twice, both times frustrated because, although they were wealthy, they were still spiritual babies (3:1).

First Corinthians was written about AD 58, partly because of the sexual immorality in the church (5:1) and also in answer to many questions they had: 7:1 – marriage. 8:1 – "Now about food sacrificed to idols." (12:1 – "Now about spiritual gifts."

He wrote his second letter to them after a "painful visit" (2:1). At the end, he said he was going to come a third time, and he was afraid he would find the same quarreling, jealousy, anger, factions, slander, gossip, arrogance, disorder, impurity, sexual sin and debauchery (12:20-13:3). He closed by saying, "Examine yourselves to see whether you are in the faith; test yourselves" (13:5).

Should we do the same?

VERSE 2
There he met _____ and her husband Aquila
Who'd recently been kicked out of _____ by Claudius
Caesar along with all the _____.

And the Beginning of the Church

VERSE 6
Paul got so exasperated with the Jews following him around everywhere causing trouble, he finally said, "Your _____ be on your own _____. From now on I will go to the _____."

VERSE 8
However, the ruler of the Synagogue did believe; and he and many of the Corinthians did what?
_____
_____

VERSE 11
How long did Paul stay here teaching? _____
_____

DAY SIX:

VERSE 17
Eventually, what did the Jews do to the former ruler of the Synagogue? _____

AD 56

VERSE 18
When Paul finally left, who did he take with him? _____ _____ and _____

VERSE 19-21
Where did they go to where Paul couldn't stay long, but promised to return to? _____

AD 57 ~ Paul's Third Missionary Trip

VERSE 24-26
While Paul was reporting to the elders in Antioch, Syria, who had sent him to be a missionary, a man named _____ arrived in Ephesus. He had a thorough knowledge of the _____ _____, but only knew the baptism

Acts of the Apostles

of John the Baptist. Who taught him in their home about Jesus having come? _____ and
_____

VERSE 28
How do we know he then became a Christian? _____
_____

Chapter 19
(Paul's Third Missionary Trip-cont.)

VERSE 1-3
When Paul arrived back in Ephesus, he found people who did not know there was a _____

VERSE 4
What was the difference between John's baptism and Jesus' baptism? (For help, refer back to Acts 2:38, the first gospel sermon.)
_____
_____
_____
_____

And the Beginning of the Church

Week Seven

Chapter 19 (cont.)
(Paul's Third Missionary Trip-cont.)

DAY ONE:

VERSE 6
Once again, because the New Testament had not been written yet, people sometimes needed external proofs. In this case, they needed to see evidence there was a _____
_____. So Paul "laid his hands on them" (something the apostles always did when imparting special spiritual gifts), and they did what? _____
_____

NOTE: The word here for "tongues" in Greek is the same word – *glossaia* -- as used to describe what the apostles did on the Day of Pentecost when everyone heard in their own language (see Acts 2:4).

VERSE 8-10
At first, Paul set up a class in the local synagogue, which lasted _____ months. But when kicked out of there, he set up another one in a lecture hall that lasted _____
_____.

VERSE 11
Who performed extraordinary miracles? _____ Name them.
_____
_____
_____
_____

VERSE 19
Eventually there was a big pagan book burning, the value of the books coming to _____ drachmas.

Acts of the Apostles

NOTE: A drachma was worth a day's wages. That would be 137 years' worth of wages burned in books that day.

VERSE 24-27
A silversmith named _____
complained Paul was ruining their business because he preached that the statues they made were _____
_____

NOTE: Artemis/Diana was the goddess of love. In her great temple at Ephesus were thousands of prostitutes who helped men "worship" this goddess. Many people made pilgrimages to Ephesus to see her temple and obtain an authentic idol to take back home with them.

VERSE 28-31
A riot started and _____ of Paul's companions were pushed _____ into the amphitheater, much like the coliseum in Rome.

Paul was talked out of going to the amphitheater by _____
_____ and _____,

VERSE 32
Why did the mob think they were at the amphitheater?
_____

DAY TWO:

VERSE 34
For how long did they shout, "Great is Artemis/Diana of the Ephesians!"? _____

VERSE 35-41
How was the city clerk able to break up the riot? _____
_____
_____

And the Beginning of the Church

Chapter 20
AD 59 ~ (Paul's Third Missionary Journey-cont.)

VERSE 6
After Paul escaped from Ephesus, he returned to Macedonia, a province in northern Greece. Then he sailed from the city of _____ and arrived at _____

NOTE: This city was formerly called Troy, and is the center of the ancient story of Helen of Troy and the Trojan Horse. In later years, it became known as Constantinople. It was supposedly also the hometown of the founders of Rome, Romulus and Remus.

VERSE 7
What was the primary purpose of their assembly on the first day of the week? To _____

What else did the early Christians do specifically on the first day of the week? (See 1 Corinthians 16:2) _____

What of significance to the church had originally happened on the first day of the week? (See Luke 24:1-7)

Since no other day of the week was significant to the Christians, what other name did it finally go by? (See Revelation 1:9-10) -

THOUGHT QUESTION: In the Old Testament, God said, "Remember THE Sabbath Day to keep it holy" (Deuteronomy 5:12-14). Which Sabbath Day did he mean? Weekly, quarterly, or yearly? The early Christians "broke bread" on THE first day of the week. Which first day of the week was it? Weekly, quarterly, or yearly?

VERSE 8-12
During Paul's sermon, what happened to Eutychus? _____

Who raised him from the dead? An ordinary Christian or an apostle?

VERSE 17

Acts of the Apostles

Then Paul set sail or Jerusalem, and at a seaport sent for the elders of the church in what city? _____

VERSE 22-23
Paul admitted to the elders that he knew what awaited him in Jerusalem. What was it?
_____
and _____

DAY THREE:

VERSE 25
In fact, Paul was convinced it would ultimately end in his
_____

VERSE 28
The elders were to do what and be what to the church?
_____
and _____

VERSE 30
Paul predicted the first heresy in the church. It would come "from your own numbers." Who was he talking to? _____
_____

NOTE: Paul, in his letter to Titus, explained that elders (plural) were to be appointed in every city (Titus 1:5), not appointed to be over several cities.

VERSE 37-38
When they prayed, everyone hugged and kissed Paul and _____ because he said he'd never _____.

NOTE: Paul wrote a letter to the church in Ephesus around AD 63 during his first imprisonment in Rome. It is a fantastic letter explaining why the world was created and how we Christians fit in to the scheme of the spirit world. I 6:12, Paul said our earthly struggle is not against flesh and blood, but powers of evil in spiritual places.

And the Beginning of the Church

Chapter 21
AD 60 ~ (Paul's Third Missionary Trip-cont.)

VERSE 4
As Paul made his way to Jerusalem, his ship stopped in Tyre, which is in today's Lebanon. What did the disciples there tell Paul?
_____
_____

VERSE 8
His ship finally docked in Caesarea where he stayed with a friend, _____, who was one of the original Seven.
What were the Seven? (See Acts 6:5) _____

VERSE 9
Philip's daughters did what? _____

NOTE: The word "prophecy" in Greek does not necessarily mean the future, though often a warning of future problems accompanied a commandment. Literally, it means "pouring out". So, prophets of God poured out his words. This is listed in 1 Corinthians 12:8-10 as one of the gifts of the Holy Spirit.

How were these gifts obtained? From apostles only. Paul, for instance, wrote the Romans in 1:11 that he wanted to see them so he could impart some spiritual gift to them. There is no one listed in the New Testament church who received a spiritual gift apart from the apostles.

THOUGHT QUESTION: Since the New Testament was not written at this time, why would prophecy be important to the first-century church?

DAY FOUR:

VERSE 12-13
What did the people of Caesarea beg Paul to do? _____
_____
What did Paul reply? _____
_____

Acts of the Apostles

VERSE 17-18
In Jerusalem, Paul went to see _____ and all the _____.

NOTE: Apparently, between Acts 15:22 and now, all the original apostles had left Jerusalem. What happened to them? According to tradition, over the next ten years, all were martyred except John:

Matthew was burned at the stake in Egypt.
Simon was crucified in Great Britain.
Peter was crucified in Rome.
Thaddeus was killed in Russia.
Andrew was crucified in Greece.
Thomas was stoned in India.
Philip was speared in Turkey.
Nathaniel was thrown into the Black Sea in Russia.

When Andrew, fisherman brother of Peter, died, it is reported that he said this:

> *Accept me, oh Christ Jesus*
> *Whom I saw,*
> *Whom I love,*
> *And in whom I am.*
> *Accept my spirit in peace*
> *In your eternal home.*

VERSE 23-24
Because the headquarters of the Jewish religion was in Jerusalem, James and the elders advised Paul to go through a Jewish ceremony to prove he didn't hate Jews. He was to do this with _____ other Jewish men.

VERSE 28-29
But some Jews, who'd followed Paul from Turkey's west-coast province of Asia, accused Paul of defiling the temple by bringing who into it? _____ Was it true?

VERSE 30
So a mob dragged Paul into the _____, closed the gates, and tried to do what to him? _____
_____

And the Beginning of the Church

VERSE 31-35
Who rescued Paul from death? _____

VERSE 38
The captain had thought Paul was the _____
Who led _____ terrorists.

DAY FIVE:

VERSE 37-40
Paul spoke to the Roman commander in what language? _____.
He then got permission to address the mob, and did so in what language? _____

Chapter 22
Paul's Trial Before the Jewish Sanhedrin

VERSE 16
In recalling his conversion, Paul said he was baptized for what reason? _____
_____

VERSE 29
When the crowd got into an uproar again, the commander ordered Paul flogged. But he was _____
to find out Paul was a _____
_____.

VERSE 30
So the commander ordered the Jewish _____
to assemble and get to the bottom of the riots.

Chapter 23
Paul's Trial Before the Jewish Sanhedrin

VERSE 1-2
Who was the high priest before whom Paul was tried? _____
_____ Who was the high priest before whom Jesus was tried? (See John 18:12-14) _____

Acts of the Apostles

NOTE: Acts 4:6 lists Ananus' (also spelled Annas and Ananias) sons as Caiaphas, John[athan], and Alexander. He had two other sons, not listed here, who Josephus says also served as high priests.

VERSE 6-8
Paul decided to 'divide and conquer" when he realized part of the Sanhedrin were Sadducees and part were Pharisees. Did it work?
_____

VERSE 10
So the Sanhedrin created a riot among themselves. It got so violent, the commander was afraid what would happen to Paul?
_____
_____

DAY SIX:

VERSE 11
That night, Jesus _____ Paul and told him he'd live to go to _____.

VERSE 12-13
The next day, _____ Jews decided to not _____ or _____ until they had _____ Paul.

VERSE 15-16
They plotted to have Paul sent back to the Sanhedrin, and on his way they would do what? _____
Who spoiled the plot? _____

VERSE 23
To protect this Roman citizen, the commander slipped Paul out of town that night under guard of _____ soldiers, _____ horsemen, and _____ spearmen, and escorted him to _____.

NOTE: Caesarea was built on the Mediterranean coast by King Herod the Great about 15 years before Jesus was born, and named after Augustus Caesar. It became Palestine's Roman (political)

71

And the Beginning of the Church

capital city, even though Jerusalem was Palestine's Jewish (religious) capital city.

VERSE 25-26
The commander sent a _____ along with the soldiers to explain that the Jews were trying to kill Paul, a Roman citizen. Who was governor of Judea at this time (the position Pilate had held during the time of Jesus)? _____

Chapter 24
AD 61 ~ Paul's Trial Before Roman Governor Felix

VERSE 2-3
The high priest hired a slick lawyer named _____ who flattered Felix by saying the Jews had enjoyed _____

NOTE: Josephus said regarding the time Felix was governor, *Now as for the affairs of the Jews, they grew worse and worse continually; for the country was again filled with robbers and impostors, who deluded the multitude. Yet did Felix catch and put to death many of those impostors every day.* (Antiquities of the Jews, Book 20, 8:5)

VERSE 5
What did Paul's enemies at this time call the church? _____
_____

Acts of the Apostles

Week Eight

Chapter 24 – (cont.)
(Paul's Trial Before Roman Governor Felix)

DAY ONE:

VERSE 14
What did Paul call the church at this time? _____
_____ (See also Acts 9:2).

Where did the early Christians get this name? (See John 14:6).

THOUGHT QUESTION: Paul intimated that this was not a sect, a denomination of the Jewish religion. Do you think we should have denominations today?

VERSE 17-19
Paul defended himself by saying
* He hadn't even been in Jerusalem for _____ years.
* He was ceremonially _____ in the temple.
* There was no _____ around him.
* The Jews from _____ weren't even in court and they were the ones who brought the original charges.

VERSE 23
Governor Felix ordered Paul be put under house arrest, so that his _____ could come see him.

VERSE 24
A few days later, Felix heard Paul again, along with his wife _____ who was a Jewess.

NOTE: Drucilla was a daughter of King Herod Agrippa, one of Herod the Great's grandsons. Josephus said the son of Felix and Drucilla was killed when Mount Vesuvius erupted in AD 79.

VERSE 26
Governor Felix often sent for Paul, hoping Paul would offer him a

And the Beginning of the Church

_____.

NOTE: During Felix's second year as governor, Claudius Caesar died, poisoned by his wife Agrippina. Then her son by a previous marriage became Caesar. His name was NERO.

VERSE 27
This went on for _____ years.

NOTE: During the time Paul was under house arrest, Felix was fighting with Jonathan, the current high priest, and one of Ananus' sons. Jonathan had wanted Caesar to make him governor instead of Felix.

Chapter 25
AD 62 ~ Paul's Trial Before Roman Governor Festus

VERSE 1
Who arrived in the province as the next governor? _____
_____

DAY TWO:

VERSE 2
Festus went immediately to the Jewish headquarters in _____ to decide what to do with Paul, still in prison.

NOTE: By this time, Herod Agrippa, king of all the Syrian and Palestinian territories, had given the high priesthood to Ismael, and the priesthood got even worse in their treatment of the people.

VERSE 3
Why did the religious leaders want Paul transferred back to Jerusalem? _____
_____

VERSE 9
When Governor Festus got to Caesarea, he held a preliminary trial. Why did he decide to send Paul back to Jerusalem? _____

Acts of the Apostles

_____

VERSE 11
Paul refused to go back to Jerusalem. Instead, he used his right as a Roman citizen and said what? _____
_____

VERSE 12
What was Governor Festus' reply? _____
_____

VERSE 13
What king arrived a few days later to visit Festus? _____
_____

VERSE 18
Festus explained to King Agrippa that Paul's accusers did not accuse him of_____
_____
_____

DAY THREE:

VERSE 19-20
Festus realized the real cause of the charges against Paul involved their religion and a man named _____ who Paul claimed _____
_____.

VERSE 23
Who accompanied King Herod Agrippa during this entire visit with Festus? _____

NOTE: Bernice was Agrippa's sister and a widow at this time. Some suspected them of incest.

VERSE 25
Preliminary to Paul's defense of himself, Festus said Paul hadn't done anything deserving of _____.

VERSE 26-27
Festus wanted King Agrippa's help in writing a _____

to Nero Caesar because it was unreasonable to send him without specifying why.

Chapter 26
Paul's Trial Before Jewish/Roman King Agrippa

VERSE 4-5
Paul said his accusers had known him _____
_____

NOTE: In Acts 22:3, Paul said that, although born in Tarsus, a city in today's Turkey, he was brought up in Jerusalem, and had been trained by Gamaliel. Acts 5:34 said Gamaliel was a member of the Sanhedrin. It was the Sanhedrin that was accusing Paul. Most of them had probably formerly been Paul's friends.

VERSE 9-10
Paul admitted he'd formerly cast Christians (saints) into prison, and
_____
_____
to put them to _____.

NOTE: This word, translated "voice" in some versions and "vote" in some versions, is from a Greek word meaning to speak out. For Paul to have been allowed a vote meant that, apparently, he had once been a member of the Sanhedrin himself, his former teacher (Gamaliel) being a senior member.

VERSE 22-23
After Paul reviewed his own conversion, he said he wasn't teaching against the Jewish religion, but was just declaring that prophecies of their religion were fulfilled in who? _____
He then declared that Jesus had done what? _____
_____

DAY FOUR:

VERSE 24
Governor Festus interrupted at this point and told Paul he was what? _____

Acts of the Apostles

VERSE 26
Paul told Festus he had no right to interrupt, because Paul had the right to _____
_____to Agrippa.

VERSE 28
What did King Agrippa reply to Paul? _____
_____
_____

NOTE: The word in Greek translated "almost" or 'shortly" indicates he was close to becoming a Christian himself.

VERSE 32
King Agrippa told the governor what things about Paul?
_____
_____

Chapter 27
AD 64 ~ Shipwreck on the Way to Rome

VERSE 2
When the writer said "we" boarded the ship, that included Paul and the writer, and perhaps others. Who was the writer? (Check Acts 1:1 and Luke 1:3) _____

VERSE 3
The ship landed at various ports, probably to pick up cargo and people. The centurion in charge of 100 soldiers allowed Paul to go ashore for what reason? _____
_____

VERSE 7-9
Why did the ship make such slow headway? _____
_____

NOTE: "The feast" referred to was the Day of Atonement that was held in October. It was too late in the season for ships to be at sea.

And the Beginning of the Church

DAY FIVE:

VERSE 12
Although the ship captain considered wintering in the harbor at Fair Havens (see v. 8), what did the ship do and why? _____
_____
_____

VERSE 13-14
What happened to threaten the ship? _____
_____

VERSE 16
What did the sailors have trouble securing on the ship? _____
_____

VERSE 17
What did the sailors do to try to hold the ship together? _____
_____

VERSE 18-19
What did they throw overboard to try to save the ship? _____
_____

VERSE 20
What did everyone on board finally conclude? _____
_____

VERSE 27
How long did the storm last? _____

DAY SIX:

VERSE 30-33
When they finally got close to shore somewhere, what did some of the sailors do, and how did the soldiers react?
_____
_____
_____

VERSE 33-38
Why did Paul urge everyone to eat? _____

Acts of the Apostles

Was he embarrassed to give thanks for the food in public? _____ How many were on board? _____

VERSE 42-43
What did the soldiers want to do before leaving the remains of their ship? _____
_____

VERSE 44
How did people get to shore? _____
_____

Chapter 28
Paul Arrives in Rome to be Heard by Nero

VERSE 1
They found out this was the island called _____

VERSE 2-6
When Paul helped build a fire, a _____ from the wood bit him. When he didn't die, what did the people decide? _____
_____

VERSE 9
What did Paul do for the people? _____
_____
Did any of the others help him perform them? _____

VERSE 11
How long did they stay on the island before setting out for Rome again? _____

VERSE 14
When they landed at Puteoli, Italy, Paul was allowed to look for whom? _____

VERSE 15
The Christian brothers heard the news and traveled to where to

And the Beginning of the Church

meet Paul? _____
_____

At the sight of the brothers from Rome, what did Paul do? _____
_____

NOTE: In Romans 1:7 & 11, Paul had written the Christians at Rome, and this letter, too, became part of the New Testament. In it he said how much he longed to see them some day. His wish was at last coming true, though not in the way he had planned.

VERSE 16
In Rome, Paul was again put under house arrest, with his own rented house, and only _____ Roman soldiers guarding him.

VERSE 17-20
When did Paul send for the Jewish leaders in Rome? _____
_____

VERSE 23
What did Paul use to try to convince the Jews that their promised Savior had come and that he was Jesus?
_____
_____
_____

VERSE 24
What was the Jews" response? _____
_____

VERSE 30
For how long was Paul under house arrest? _____
_____

THOUGHT QUESTION: How has this book of the Bible affected your life? _____
_____
_____
_____

Thank You

Thanks for reading my book! I'm so honored that you chose to spend your precious time with my research. You are appreciated. I'm an author who relies on my readers to help spread the word about stories you enjoy and facts you discover. Would you take a few minutes to let your friends know on Facebook, Pinterest... wherever you go online?

Also, each honest review on bookseller websites means a lot to me and helps other readers know if this is a book they might enjoy.

About The Author

Katheryn Maddox Haddad grew up in northern USA and now lives in India, where she doesn't have to shovel sunshine. She basks in 100-degree weather with banana trees, monkeys, and a computer with most of the letters worn off.

Besides the US and India, she has lived in four other countries ~ Korea, Canada, Afghanistan, and Abu Dhabi, and has made short visits to Tokyo and Sri Lanka.

With a bachelor's degree in English, Bible, and social science from Harding University and part of a master's degree in Bible from the Harding Graduate School of Theology (including Greek), she also has a master's degree in human relations from Abilene Christian University.

She spends half her day writing and the other half teaching English over the internet worldwide using the Bible as a textbook. She has taught nearly 10,000 Muslims over 15 years in the Middle East. Students she has converted to Christianity are in hiding in Afghanistan, Iran, Iraq, Yemen, Jordan, Uzbekistan, Tajikistan, and Palestine. "They are my heroes," she declares.

Currently, she also teaches Bible history at the MH School of Theology in Punadipadu, Krishna, Andhra Pradesh, India.

She is a member of American Christian Fiction Writers, the American Historical Association, World History Association, World Archaeological College, Association of Ancient Historians, and Archaeological Research Institute.

Oh, and for her next birthday, she plans to ride an elephant.

Connect With the Author

FACEBOOK

I welcome contact from readers, which you can do here:

Pictorial INDEX to all books & categories
Website: https://NorthernLightsPublishingHouse.com
Come read a sample chapter of each book

Facebook JUST ME Profile:
https://www.facebook.com/ReadsForAllAges/
Daily inspiration, poster, & prayer

Facebook BOOKS Page
https://www.facebook.com/katheryn.maddox.haddad/
Get in on weekly discounts only known by you

PINTEREST
https://www.pinterest.com/haddad1940/

YOUTUBE
https://www.youtube.com/@KH-bi3fr

email: khaddad1940@gmail.com

And the Beginning of the Church

Buy Your Next Book Now

BIBLICAL HISTORICAL NOVELS
Series of 8: Soul Journey With the Real Jesus
Ongoing Series of 8: Intrepid Men of God

CHILDREN'S BIBLE STORYBOOKS
Series of 8: A Child's Life of Christ
Series of 10: A Child's Bible Heroes
Series of 8: A Child's Bible Kids

WORLDWIDE HISTORICAL RESEARCH
DOCUMENTARY, THESIS, NOVEL & SCREENPLAY WRITERS

BIBLE TOPICS
Applied Christianity: Handbook 500 Good Works
Christianity or Islam? The Contrast
The Holy Spirit: 592 Verses Examined
Inside the Hearts of Bible Women-Reader+Audio+Leader
Revelation: A Love Letter From God
Worship Changes Since 1st Century + Worship 1st Century Way
Was Jesus God? (Why Evil)
365 Life-Changing Scriptures Day by Date
The Road to Heaven
The Lord's Supper: 52 Readings with Prayers

BIBLE FUN BOOKS
Bible Puzzles, Bible Song Book, Bible Numbers

TOUCHING GOD SERIES
365 Golden Bible Thoughts: God's Heart to Yours
365 Pearls of Wisdom: God's Soul to Yours
365 Silver-Winged Prayers: Your Spirit to God's

SURVEY SERIES: EASY BIBLE WORKBOOKS
→Old Testament & New Testament Surveys
→Questions You Have Asked-Part I & II

Genealogy: How to Climb Your Family Tree Without Falling Out
Volume I & 2: Beginner-Intermediate & Colonial-Medieval

Genealogy: How to Climb Your Family Tree Without Falling Out
Volume I & 2: Beginner-Intermediate & Colonial-Medieval

www.ingramcontent.com/pod-product-compliance
Lightning Source LLC
Chambersburg PA
CBHW071327040426
42444CB00009B/2102